WORLD'S FAVORITE

Selected Violin Pieces

including

ABEILLE, L' (THE BEE)
ADAGIO ("MOONLIGHT" SONATA)

ARAGONAISE

CARO MIO BEN (AIR)

CHANSON TRISTE

LOURE

MINUET IN G
MINUET L'ANTIQUE
"MINUTE" WALTZ

MOTO PERPETUO (THE RAIN)

NORWEGIAN DANCE

PIZZICATO ("SYLVIA" BALLET)

POUPÉE VALSANTE (WALTZING DOLL)

SCARF DANCE

SOUVENIR

VALSETTE

— PLUS —

Phantasies for Unaccompanied Violin by Georg Philipp Telemann

edited by Robert Kail

for ASHLEY PUBLICATIONS

Copyright © 1983 by Ashley Publications, Inc., 263 Veterans Blvd., Carlstadt, N.J. 07072, U.S.A.

CONTENTS

— PLUS —
Phantasies for Unaccompanied Violin
by Georg Philipp Telemann

Andante

C. W. GLUCK

L' Abeille
(The Bee)

FRANÇOIS SCHUBERT

Adagio

(From "Moonlight" Sonata)

L. VAN BEETHOVEN

Air
(Pur dicesti)

ANTONIO LOTTI

Allegretto grazioso

Andante
(From Violin Concerto)

RICHARD STRAUSS, Op. 8

Lento ma non troppo

14

Minuet L'Antique

I. J. PADEREWSKI

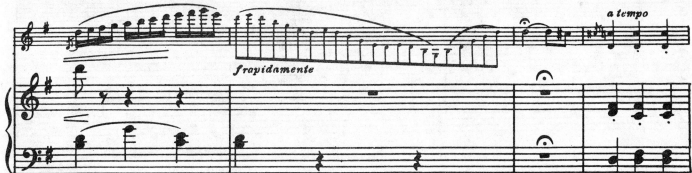

CODA
Vivo

Aragonaise

Azzez animé et trèz brillant

JULES MASSENET

Berceuse

Allegretto tranquillo

EDWARD GRIEG

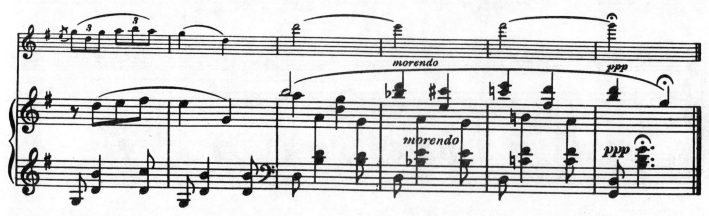

Bourrée

G. F. HANDEL

Allegretto

p espressivo

p

Consolation

FR. LISZT

Aria
(Caro mio ben)

G. GIORDANI

Larghetto

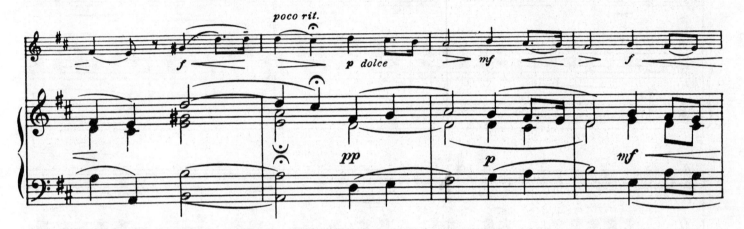

An den Frühling

(To Spring)

EDWARD GRIEG

Allegro appassionato

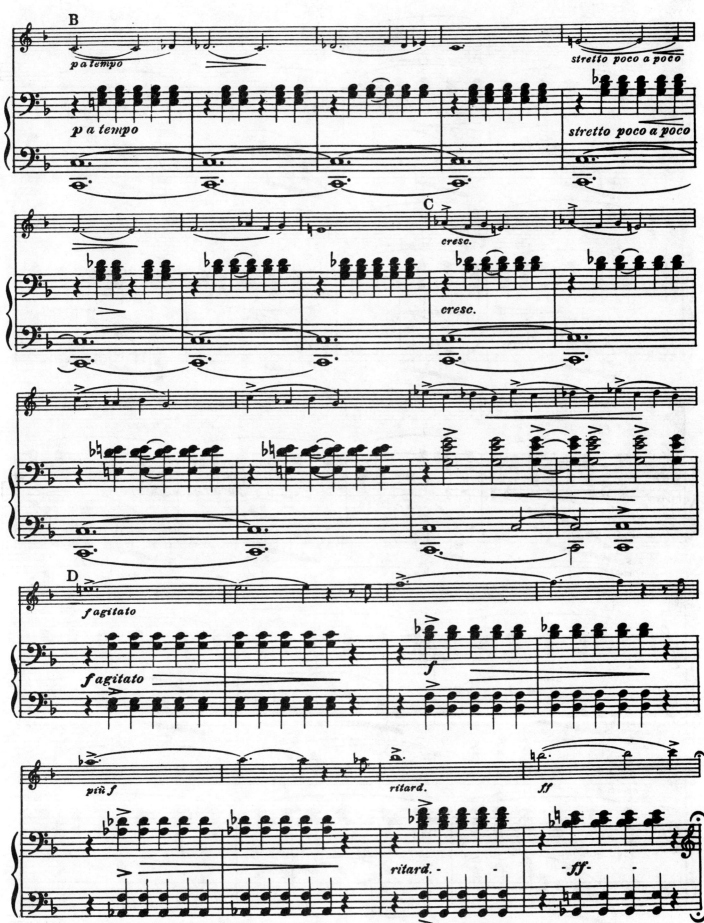

Tempo I

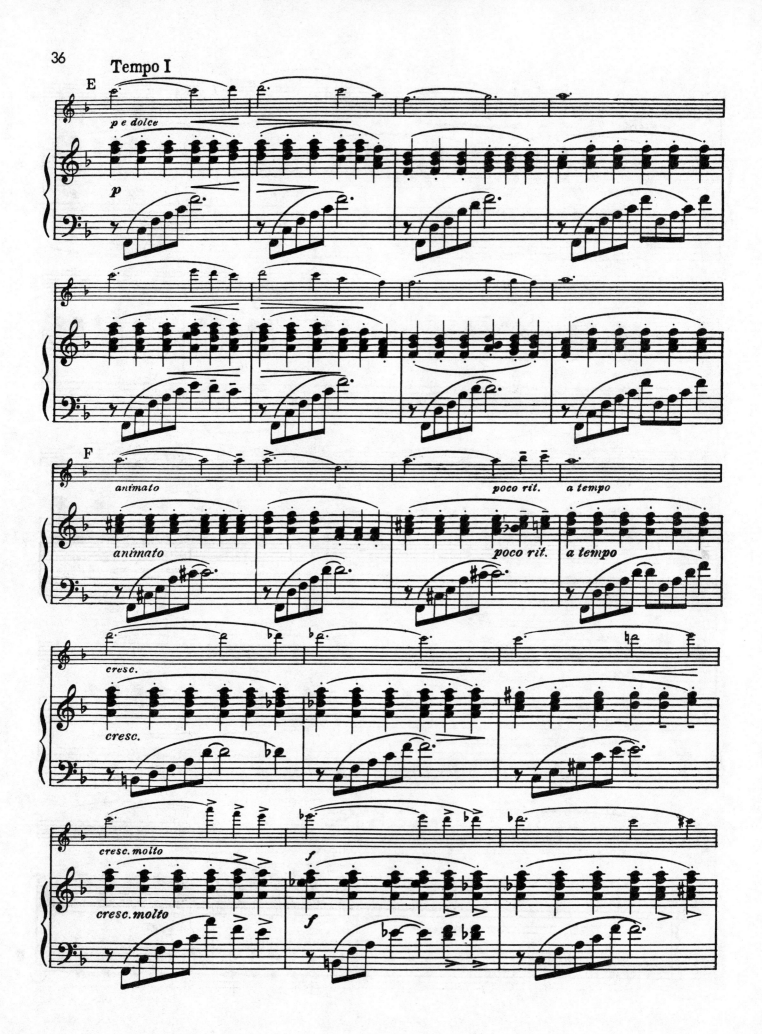

Chanson Triste

P. TSCHAIKOWSKY

Allegro non troppo

Élégie
Mélodie

JULES MASSENET

Lento espressivo

Scarf Dance

CÉCILE CHAMINADE

Longing For Home
(Heimweh)

A. JUNGMANN

Loure

J. S. BACH

Allegro moderato

D.C. al Fine

Mazurka

FR. CHOPIN. Op.7 № 1

Minuet in G

L. VAN BEETHOVEN

TRIO

mf *bouncing stroke* *mf*

f

Minuet D.C.

Minuet D.C.

Andante religioso

Andante

FRANCIS THOMÉ

Largamente

Tempo I

"Minute" Waltz

Molto vivace
risoluto

FR. CHOPIN. Op. 64. N⁰ 1

Nachtstück

R. SCHUMANN, Op. 23, № 4

Tempo I

The Rain
(Perpetuum Mobile)

CARL BOHM

Allegretto

Special Note - As originally written, the violin part of this composition is played in sixteenth notes, but a very pretty effect is gained by doubling the sixteenths.

Norwegian Dance

EDWARD GRIEG

Allegretto tranquillo e grazioso

Valsette

FÉLIX BOROWSKI

Tempo Primo

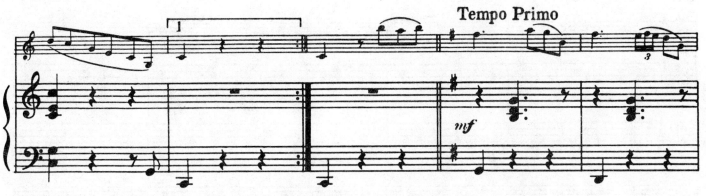

Orientale
(From "The Kaleidescope")

CÈSAR CUI. Op. 50

Allegretto

Salut d'Amour
(Love's Greeting)

EDWARD ELGAR

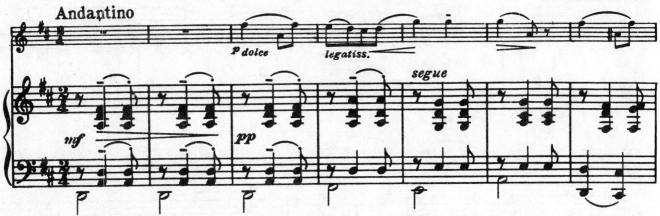

Pizzicato

(From "Sylvia" Ballet)

L. DELIBES

Un poco più anima

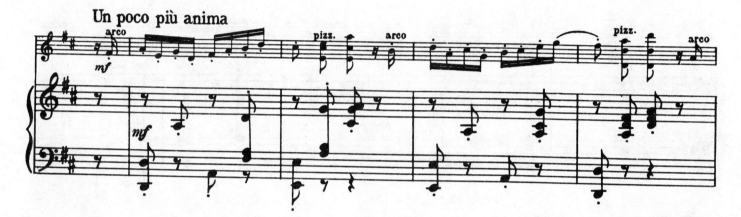

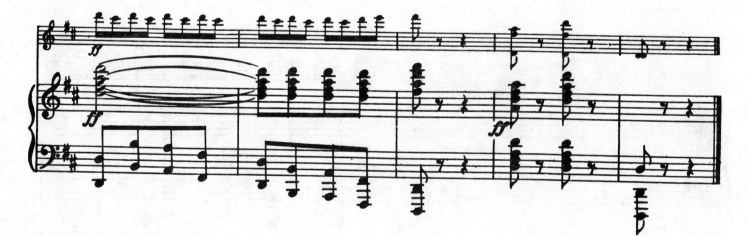

La Zingana
(Hungarian Mazurka)

CARL BOHM

Poupée Valsante

(Waltzing Doll)

EDWARD POLDINI

Tempo di Valse

Rêverie

CLAUDE DEBUSSY

Tempo Primo

Più lento

Romance

A. RUBINSTEIN, Op. 44

Andante con moto

Souvenir

FRANZ DRDLA

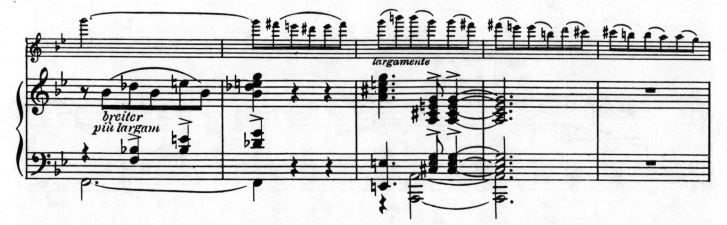

Idyl

E. MACDOWELL, Op. 28, N⁰ 1

Allegretto quasi andantino

Sérénade

G. PIERNÉ

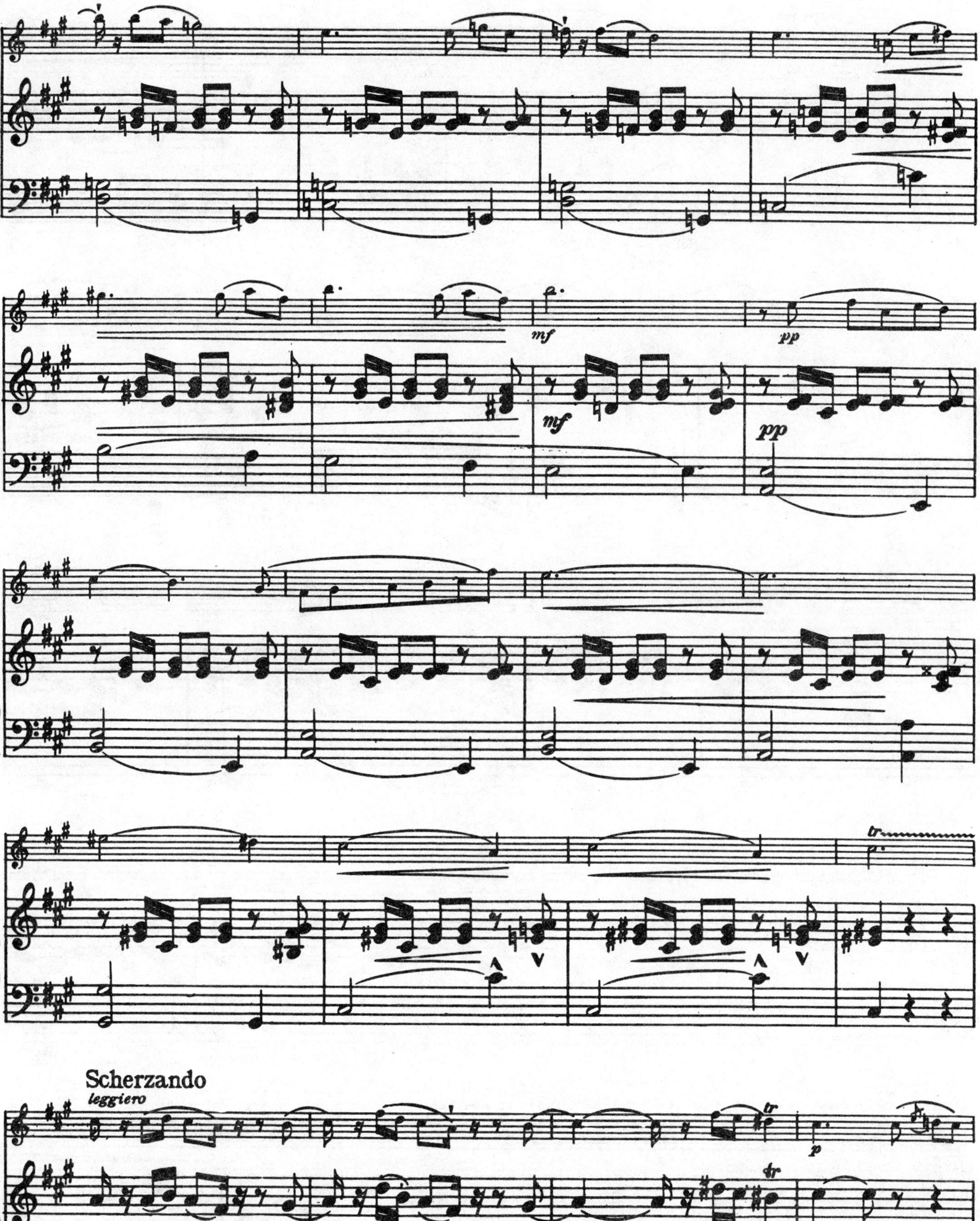
mf
mf
pp
pp
Scherzando
leggiero
leggiero
tr
p

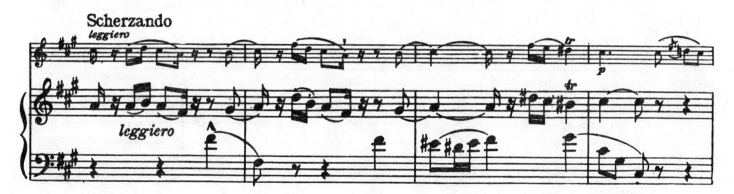

Polish Dance

X. SCHARWENKA. Op. 3, № 1

Con fuoco

112

WORLD'S FAVORITE

Selected Violin Pieces

including

ABEILLE, L' (THE BEE)
ADAGIO ("MOONLIGHT" SONATA)

ARAGONAISE

CARO MIO BEN (AIR)

CHANSON TRISTE

LOURE

MINUET IN G
MINUET L'ANTIQUE
"MINUTE" WALTZ

MOTO PERPETUO (THE RAIN)

NORWEGIAN DANCE

PIZZICATO ("SYLVIA" BALLET)

POUPÉE VALSANTE (WALTZING DOLL)

SCARF DANCE

SOUVENIR.

VALSETTE

— PLUS —

Phantasies for Unaccompanied Violin by Georg Philipp Telemann

edited by Robert Kail

for ASHLEY PUBLICATIONS

CONTENTS

— PLUS —
Phantasies for Unaccompanied Violin
by Georg Philipp Telemann

Scarf Dance

CÉCILE CHAMINADE

L'Abeille

(The Bee)

FRANÇOIS SCHUBERT

Adagio
(From "Moonlight" Sonata)

L. VAN BEETHOVEN

Air
(Pur Dicesti)

ANTONIO LOTTI

Loure

J. S. BACH

Andante

C.W. GLUCK

Andante
(From Violin Concerto)

RICHARD STRAUSS, Op. 8

Lento ma non troppo

Andante Religioso

FRANCIS THOMÉ

Aragonaise

J. MASSENET

Assez animé et trés brillant

En animant peu á peu

Tempo Primo animé

Berceuse

EDWARD GRIEG

La Zingana
(Hungarian Mazurka)

CARL BOHM

Bourrée

G. F. HANDEL

Allegretto

Chanson Triste

Allegro non troppo

P. TSCHAIKOWSKY

Consolation

FR. LISZT

Élégie

(Mélodie)

JULES MASSENET

Minuet in G

L. van BEETHOVEN

Aria
(Caro mio ben)

G. GIORDANI

Idyl

Allegretto quasi Andantino

E. MACDOWELL, Op. 28

Longing For Home
(Heimwch)

A. JUNGMANN

Mazurka

FR. CHOPIN, Op. 7. N° 1

Minuet L'Antique

I. J. PADEREWSKI

"Minute" Waltz

Molto vivace
risoluto

FR. CHOPIN, Op. 64. No 1

cresc. poco a poco -

The Rain
(Perpetuum Mobile)

CARL BOHM

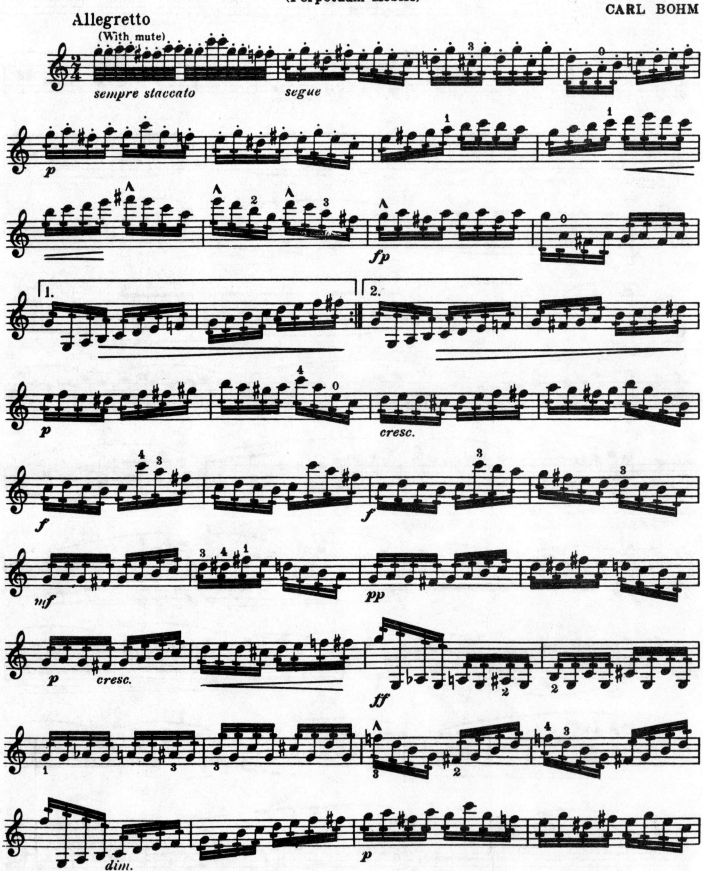

Special Note- As originally written, the violin part of this composition is played in sixteenth notes, but a very pretty effect is gained by doubling the sixteenths.

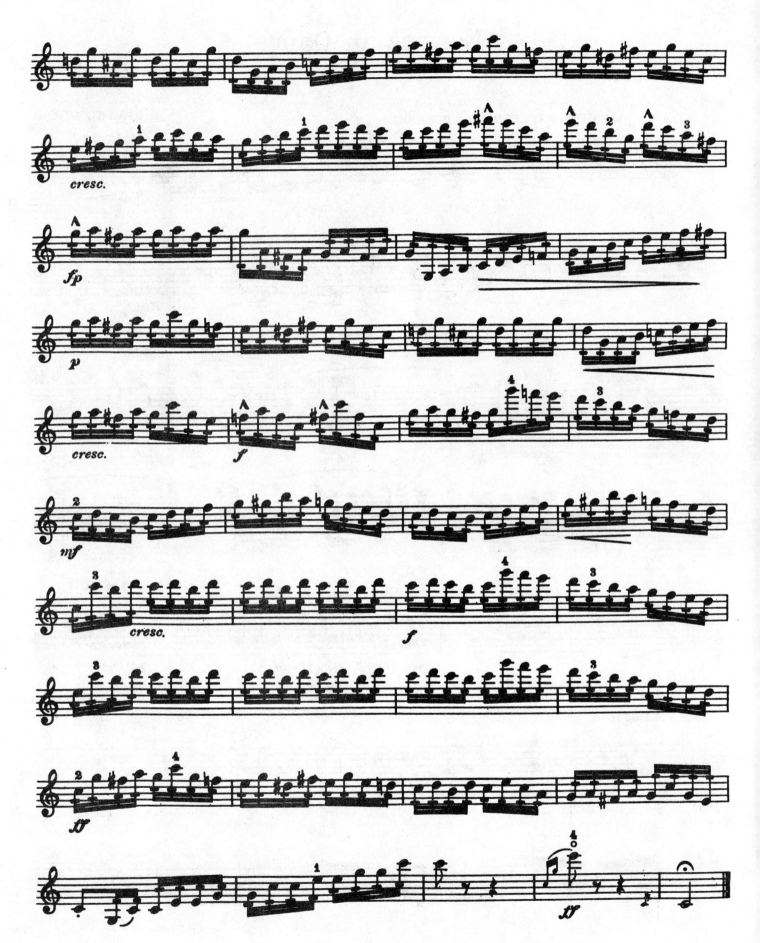

Norwegian Dance

Allegretto tranquillo e grazioso

EDWARD GRIEG

Nachtstück

R. SCHUMANN, Op. 23, № 4

Orientale

(From "The Kaleidescope")

CÉSAR CUI, Op. 50

Pizzicato

(From "Sylvia" Ballet)

L. DELIBES

Un poco più anima.

Polish Dance

Con fuoco

X. SCHARWENKA, Op. 3, № 1

Poupée Valsante
(Waltzing Doll)

ED. POLDINI

Tempo di Valse

Tempo Primo

Rêverie

CLAUDE DEBUSSY

Romance

Andante con moto

A. RUBINSTEIN, Op. 44

Salut d'Amour
(Love's Greeting)

EDWARD ELGAR

Sérénade

G. PIERNÉ

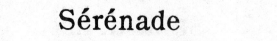

Souvenir

FRANZ DRDLA

Note — The Mark II indicates a slight pause.

Valsette

FÉLIX BOROWSKI

Animato

Fantasie per il Violino senza Basso

FANTASIA I

Georg Philipp Telemann
(1681-1767)

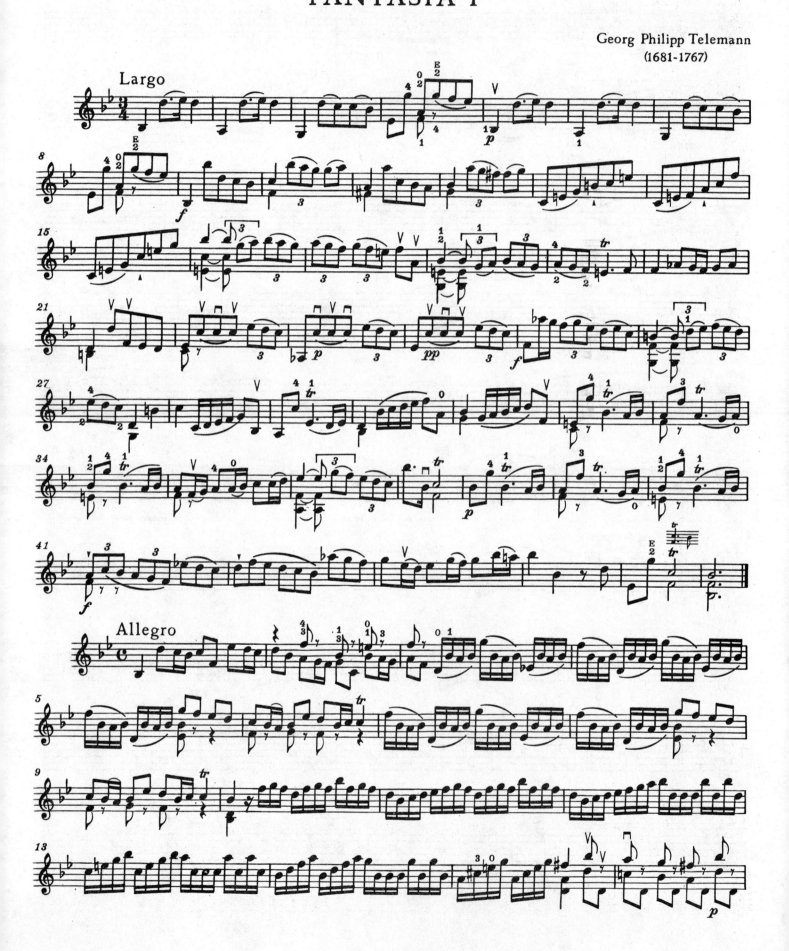

Si replica l'allegro

FANTASIA III

57

FANTASIA VII

FANTASIA IX

FANTASIA XII

An den Frühling
(To Spring)

EDWARD GRIEG